I Got the Power

B.A.D. Decisions Companion Journal

© 2024 Alisa L. Grace

All rights reserved.

No part of this book may be reproduced in any form or by any electronic or mechanical means, including information storage and retrieval systems, without permission in writing from the publisher.

Self-Published by

Alisa L. Grace

Sanford, FL 32771

ISBN: 978-1-966129-60-8

First Edition

Printed in the United States of America

Dear Amazing Middle Schooler,

Congratulations on taking charge of your life with "I Got the Power: B.A.D. Decisions!" It's time to turn those powerful ideas into action with this incredible companion journal.

This isn't just any old notebook – it's your secret weapon for making those B.A.D. Decisions stick! Think of it as your personal training ground for mastering your mind, achieving your goals, and building a life you love. It's a **12-week journey** designed to guide you step-by-step as you learn to flex your "B.A.D. Decision" muscles.

Here's how this companion journal will help you:

> **Dive deeper:** Explore the ideas from the book in more detail and make them your own.
>
> **Track your progress:** Celebrate your wins, learn from your challenges, and see how far you've come.
>
> **Make it personal:** Reflect on your unique experiences, set personalized goals, and create a plan that works for YOU.
>
> **Boost your confidence:** Each week, you'll learn a new affirmation to practice daily, building your self-belief and empowering you to achieve your dreams.
>
> **Keep the momentum going:** This journal is your space to continue growing and learning long after you finish reading the book.

Inside these pages, you'll discover:

> **Weekly challenges:** Fun and engaging activities to help you practice mindfulness, set SMART goals, build healthy habits, and manage your time like a pro.

Affirmation Power-Ups: A weekly affirmation to inspire you and boost your confidence.

Journaling prompts: Thought-provoking questions to inspire self-reflection, explore your feelings, and unleash your creativity.

Space for your ideas: Plenty of room to jot down your thoughts, dreams, and plans for the future.

Inspiration and encouragement: Motivational quotes and reminders to keep you going on your B.A.D. Decisions journey.

This companion journal is your partner in crime, your personal cheerleader, and guide to unlocking your full potential. So grab your favorite pen, find a quiet corner, and get ready to be transformed over the next 12 weeks!

Your Coach and Guide,

Alisa L. Grace

Author of "I Got the Power: B.A.D. Decisions"

My B.A.D. Decisions Launchpad

About Me:

My Name: _____

My Age: _____

My Favorite Things: _____

My Dreams for the Future: _____

Why I'm Excited to Use This Journal:

I want to learn how to: _____
_____

I want to get better at: _____
_____

I'm hoping this journal will help me: _____
_____

Self-Portrait

My B.A.D. Decisions Goals:

Brainpower: (What do you want to achieve with mindfulness and positive thinking?)

- *Example: I want to learn how to calm my mind when I feel stressed.*

Actionable Steps: (What goals do you want to set and achieve?)

- *Example: I want to improve my grades in math.*

Disciplined Determination: (What healthy habits do you want to build?)

- *Example: I want to get more sleep and exercise regularly.*

My Message to Myself:

(This is a space for students to write a message of encouragement to themselves.)

Example: *I know you can do this! You are strong, capable, and amazing. Believe in yourself and never give up on your dreams!*

My B.A.D. Decisions Action Plan:

This is your command center for making extraordinary things happen! Each week, you'll focus on one specific goal, build a healthy habit, and try a mindfulness technique. You'll also have a special "Affirmation Power-Up" to boost your confidence and motivate you.

Think of it like this:

> **Goal Setting:** You choose a target and create a plan to hit it. What do you want to achieve this week? It could be anything from acing a test to learning a new skill to being a better friend.
>
> **Habit Formation:** This is where you train your brain to do incredible things automatically. Want to get more sleep? Read more books? Eat healthier snacks? This is where you make it happen.
>
> **Time Management:** This is where you become a master of time, juggling schoolwork, activities, and fun without feeling overwhelmed. You'll learn to prioritize, schedule, and conquer procrastination.
>
> **Mindfulness Practice:** This is where you train your mind to be calm, focused, and present. You'll learn techniques to quiet your "Thought Monster" and find your inner peace.
>
> **Weekly Affirmation Power-Up:** This is your secret weapon for building self-belief. Each week, you'll have a unique affirmation to write down and repeat to yourself daily. These positive statements will help you overcome challenges and achieve your dreams.

Ready to take charge? Let's do this!

Week 1:

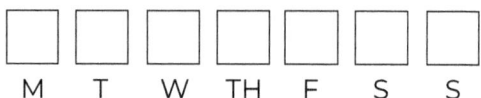

| M | T | W | TH | F | S | S |

Weekly Affirmation Power-Up:
I am capable of amazing things!
(Write it down every day this week and repeat it to yourself often.)

1. Goal Setting:

My Top Goal This Week: (Choose one goal to focus on first.)

_____

_____

Why is this goal important to me?

_____

_____

My SMART Plan:

- **S**pecific: (What exactly will I do?)

  _____

  _____

- **M**easurable: (How will I track my progress?)

  _____

  _____

- **A**chievable: (Is this goal realistic for me?)

  _____

  _____

- **R**elevant: (Does this goal align with my values and interests?)

  _____

  _____

- **T**ime-bound: (What is my deadline?)

  _____

  _____

Potential Obstacles: (What might get in my way?)

_____

_____

Solutions: (How will I overcome these obstacles?)

_____

_____

2. Habit Formation:

Habit I want to build this week: (e.g., exercise more, read every day, get enough sleep)

_____

_____

My Plan: (How will I make this habit a part of my routine?)

_____

_____

Tracking: (I will track my progress by...)

_____

_____

3. Time Management:

My Weekly Schedule: (I will create a schedule for my week that includes...)

_____

_____

My To-Do List: (My top 3 priorities this week are...)

1. _____

2. _____

3. _____

Time-Saving Tip: (One strategy I will use to be more efficient with my time is...)

_____

_____

4. Mindfulness Practice:

Mindfulness Technique I will try this week: (e.g., mindful breathing, body scan, mindful walking)

_____

_____

When and where will I practice? (e.g., before bed in my room, during my lunch break)

_____

_____

Week 2 :

Weekly Affirmation Power-Up:
I am brave and I can overcome any challenge.
(Write it down every day this week and repeat it to yourself often.)

1. Goal Setting:

My Top Goal This Week: (Choose one goal to focus on first.)

_____

_____

Why is this goal important to me?

_____

_____

My SMART Plan:

- **S**pecific: (What exactly will I do?)

  _____

  _____

- **M**easurable: (How will I track my progress?)

  _____

  _____

- **A**chievable: (Is this goal realistic for me?)

  _____

  _____

- **R**elevant: (Does this goal align with my values and interests?)

  _____

  _____

- **T**ime-bound: (What is my deadline?)

  _____

  _____

Potential Obstacles: (What might get in my way?)

_____

_____

Solutions: (How will I overcome these obstacles?)

_____

_____

2. Habit Formation:

Habit I want to build this week: (e.g., exercise more, read every day, get enough sleep)

_____

_____

My Plan: (How will I make this habit a part of my routine?)

_____

_____

Tracking: (I will track my progress by...)

_____

_____

3. Time Management:

My Weekly Schedule: (I will create a schedule for my week that includes...)

_____

_____

My To-Do List: (My top 3 priorities this week are...)

1. _____

2. _____

3. _____

Time-Saving Tip: (One strategy I will use to be more efficient with my time is...)

_____

_____

4. Mindfulness Practice:

Mindfulness Technique I will try this week: (e.g., mindful breathing, body scan, mindful walking)

_____

_____

When and where will I practice? (e.g., before bed in my room, during my lunch break)

_____

_____

Week 3:

Weekly Affirmation Power-Up:
I am kind to myself and others.
(Write it down every day this week and repeat it to yourself often.)

1. Goal Setting:

My Top Goal This Week: (Choose one goal to focus on first.)

_____

_____

Why is this goal important to me?

_____

_____

My SMART Plan:

- **S**pecific: (What exactly will I do?)

  _____

  _____

- **M**easurable: (How will I track my progress?)

  _____

  _____

- **A**chievable: (Is this goal realistic for me?)

  _____

  _____

- **R**elevant: (Does this goal align with my values and interests?)

  _____

  _____

- **T**ime-bound: (What is my deadline?)

  _____

  _____

Potential Obstacles: (What might get in my way?)

_____

_____

Solutions: (How will I overcome these obstacles?)

_____

_____

2. Habit Formation:

Habit I want to build this week: (e.g., exercise more, read every day, get enough sleep)

_____

_____

My Plan: (How will I make this habit a part of my routine?)

_____

_____

Tracking: (I will track my progress by...)

_____

_____

3. Time Management:

My Weekly Schedule: (I will create a schedule for my week that includes...)

_____

_____

My To-Do List: (My top 3 priorities this week are...)

1. _____

2. _____

3. _____

Time-Saving Tip: (One strategy I will use to be more efficient with my time is...)

_____

_____

4. Mindfulness Practice:

Mindfulness Technique I will try this week: (e.g., mindful breathing, body scan, mindful walking)

_____

_____

When and where will I practice? (e.g., before bed in my room, during my lunch break)

_____

_____

Week 3: Keep Going!

Hey Awesome You,

How's it going with your B.A.D. Decisions journey? I just wanted to drop you a quick note to say keep up the amazing work!

I know it's not always easy to stick to your goals, build new habits, and find time for mindfulness. But every small step you take is a victory! Remember to celebrate your wins, no matter how small they seem.

Don't be afraid to ask for help if you need it. Talk to a trusted friend, family member, teacher, or counselor. They can offer support, encouragement, and guidance along the way.

And most importantly, believe in yourself! You have the power to achieve incredible things.

Keep shining bright,

Coach Grace

Week 4:

Weekly Affirmation Power-Up:
II am grateful for all the good things in my life.
(Write it down every day this week and repeat it to yourself often.)

1. Goal Setting:

My Top Goal This Week: (Choose one goal to focus on first.)

_____

_____

Why is this goal important to me?

_____

_____

My SMART Plan:

- **S**pecific: (What exactly will I do?)

  _____

  _____

- **M**easurable: (How will I track my progress?)

  _____

  _____

- **A**chievable: (Is this goal realistic for me?)

  _____

  _____

- **R**elevant: (Does this goal align with my values and interests?)

  _____

  _____

- **T**ime-bound: (What is my deadline?)

  _____

  _____

Potential Obstacles: (What might get in my way?)

_____

_____

Solutions: (How will I overcome these obstacles?)

_____

_____

2. Habit Formation:

Habit I want to build this week: (e.g., exercise more, read every day, get enough sleep)

_____

_____

My Plan: (How will I make this habit a part of my routine?)

_____

_____

Tracking: (I will track my progress by...)

_____

_____

3. Time Management:

My Weekly Schedule: (I will create a schedule for my week that includes...)

_____

_____

My To-Do List: (My top 3 priorities this week are...)

1. _____

2. _____

3. _____

Time-Saving Tip: (One strategy I will use to be more efficient with my time is...)

_____

_____

4. Mindfulness Practice:

Mindfulness Technique I will try this week: (e.g., mindful breathing, body scan, mindful walking)

_____

_____

When and where will I practice? (e.g., before bed in my room, during my lunch break)

_____

_____

Week 5:

Weekly Affirmation Power-Up:
I am creative and I love to learn new things.
(Write it down every day this week and repeat it to yourself often.)

1. Goal Setting:

My Top Goal This Week: (Choose one goal to focus on first.)

_____

_____

Why is this goal important to me?

_____

_____

My SMART Plan:

- **S**pecific: (What exactly will I do?)

  _____

  _____

- **M**easurable: (How will I track my progress?)

  _____

  _____

- **A**chievable: (Is this goal realistic for me?)

  _____

  _____

- **R**elevant: (Does this goal align with my values and interests?)

  _____

  _____

- **T**ime-bound: (What is my deadline?)

  _____

  _____

Potential Obstacles: (What might get in my way?)

_____

_____

Solutions: (How will I overcome these obstacles?)

_____

_____

2. Habit Formation:

Habit I want to build this week: (e.g., exercise more, read every day, get enough sleep)

_____

_____

My Plan: (How will I make this habit a part of my routine?)

_____

_____

Tracking: (I will track my progress by...)

_____

_____

3. Time Management:

My Weekly Schedule: (I will create a schedule for my week that includes...)

_____

_____

My To-Do List: (My top 3 priorities this week are...)

1. _____

2. _____

3. _____

Time-Saving Tip: (One strategy I will use to be more efficient with my time is...)

_____

_____

4. Mindfulness Practice:

Mindfulness Technique I will try this week: (e.g., mindful breathing, body scan, mindful walking)

_____

_____

When and where will I practice? (e.g., before bed in my room, during my lunch break)

_____

_____

Week 6:

M T W TH F S S

Weekly Affirmation Power-Up:
I am worthy of love and respect
(Write it down every day this week and repeat it to yourself often.)

1. Goal Setting:

My Top Goal This Week: (Choose one goal to focus on first.)

_____

_____

Why is this goal important to me?

_____

_____

My SMART Plan:

- **S**pecific: (What exactly will I do?)

  _____

  _____

- **M**easurable: (How will I track my progress?)

  _____

  _____

- **A**chievable: (Is this goal realistic for me?)

  _____

  _____

- **R**elevant: (Does this goal align with my values and interests?)

  _____

  _____

- **T**ime-bound: (What is my deadline?)

  _____

  _____

Potential Obstacles: (What might get in my way?)

_____

_____

Solutions: (How will I overcome these obstacles?)

_____

_____

2. Habit Formation:

Habit I want to build this week: (e.g., exercise more, read every day, get enough sleep)

_____

_____

My Plan: (How will I make this habit a part of my routine?)

_____

_____

Tracking: (I will track my progress by...)

_____

_____

3. Time Management:

My Weekly Schedule: (I will create a schedule for my week that includes...)

_____

_____

My To-Do List: (My top 3 priorities this week are...)

1. _____

2. _____

3. _____

Time-Saving Tip: (One strategy I will use to be more efficient with my time is...)

_____

_____

4. Mindfulness Practice:

Mindfulness Technique I will try this week: (e.g., mindful breathing, body scan, mindful walking)

_____

_____

When and where will I practice? (e.g., before bed in my room, during my lunch break)

_____

_____

Week 6: You're Halfway There!

Woohoo! You're halfway through your 12-week B.A.D. Decisions journey!

Take a moment to reflect on how far you've come. What have you learned about yourself? What challenges have you overcome? What are you most proud of?

Remember, this is a marathon, not a sprint. It's okay to have ups and downs along the way. Just keep focusing on your goals, practicing healthy habits, and believing in your amazing potential.

You're doing great!

Cheers,

Coach Grace

Week 7:

M   T   W   TH   F   S   S

Weekly Affirmation Power-Up:
I am strong and resilient.
(Write it down every day this week and repeat it to yourself often.)

1. Goal Setting:

My Top Goal This Week: (Choose one goal to focus on first.)

_____

_____

Why is this goal important to me?

_____

_____

My SMART Plan:

- **S**pecific: (What exactly will I do?)

  _____

  _____

- **M**easurable: (How will I track my progress?)

  _____

  _____

- **A**chievable: (Is this goal realistic for me?)

  _____

  _____

- **R**elevant: (Does this goal align with my values and interests?)

  _____

  _____

- **T**ime-bound: (What is my deadline?)

  _____

  _____

Potential Obstacles: (What might get in my way?)

_____

_____

Solutions: (How will I overcome these obstacles?)

_____

_____

2. Habit Formation:

Habit I want to build this week: (e.g., exercise more, read every day, get enough sleep)

_____

_____

My Plan: (How will I make this habit a part of my routine?)

_____

_____

Tracking: (I will track my progress by...)

_____

_____

3. Time Management:

My Weekly Schedule: (I will create a schedule for my week that includes...)

_____

_____

My To-Do List: (My top 3 priorities this week are...)

1. _____

2. _____

3. _____

Time-Saving Tip: (One strategy I will use to be more efficient with my time is...)

_____

_____

4. Mindfulness Practice:

Mindfulness Technique I will try this week: (e.g., mindful breathing, body scan, mindful walking)

_____

_____

When and where will I practice? (e.g., before bed in my room, during my lunch break)

_____

_____

Week 8:

Weekly Affirmation Power-Up:
I am unique and special.
(Write it down every day this week and repeat it to yourself often.)

1. Goal Setting:

My Top Goal This Week: (Choose one goal to focus on first.)

_____
_____

Why is this goal important to me?

_____
_____

My SMART Plan:

- **S**pecific: (What exactly will I do?)

  _____

  _____

- **M**easurable: (How will I track my progress?)

  _____

  _____

- **A**chievable: (Is this goal realistic for me?)

  _____

  _____

- **R**elevant: (Does this goal align with my values and interests?)

  _____

  _____

- **T**ime-bound: (What is my deadline?)

  _____

  _____

Potential Obstacles: (What might get in my way?)

_____

_____

Solutions: (How will I overcome these obstacles?)

_____

_____

2. Habit Formation:

Habit I want to build this week: (e.g., exercise more, read every day, get enough sleep)

_____

_____

My Plan: (How will I make this habit a part of my routine?)

_____

_____

Tracking: (I will track my progress by...)

_____
_____

3. Time Management:

My Weekly Schedule: (I will create a schedule for my week that includes...)

_____
_____

My To-Do List: (My top 3 priorities this week are...)

1. _____
2. _____
3. _____

Time-Saving Tip: (One strategy I will use to be more efficient with my time is...)

_____
_____

4. Mindfulness Practice:

Mindfulness Technique I will try this week: (e.g., mindful breathing, body scan, mindful walking)

_____

_____

When and where will I practice? (e.g., before bed in my room, during my lunch break)

_____

_____

Week 9:

Weekly Affirmation Power-Up:
I am capable of achieving my dreams.
(Write it down every day this week and repeat it to yourself often.)

1. Goal Setting:

My Top Goal This Week: (Choose one goal to focus on first.)

_____

_____

Why is this goal important to me?

_____

_____

My SMART Plan:

- **S**pecific: (What exactly will I do?)

  _____

  _____

- **M**easurable: (How will I track my progress?)

  _____

  _____

- **A**chievable: (Is this goal realistic for me?)

  _____

  _____

- **R**elevant: (Does this goal align with my values and interests?)

  _____

  _____

- **T**ime-bound: (What is my deadline?)

  _____

  _____

Potential Obstacles: (What might get in my way?)

_____

_____

Solutions: (How will I overcome these obstacles?)

_____

_____

2. Habit Formation:

Habit I want to build this week: (e.g., exercise more, read every day, get enough sleep)

_____

_____

My Plan: (How will I make this habit a part of my routine?)

_____

_____

Tracking: (I will track my progress by...)

_____

_____

3. Time Management:

My Weekly Schedule: (I will create a schedule for my week that includes...)

_____

_____

My To-Do List: (My top 3 priorities this week are...)

1. _____

2. _____

3. _____

Time-Saving Tip: (One strategy I will use to be more efficient with my time is...)

_____

_____

4. Mindfulness Practice:

Mindfulness Technique I will try this week: (e.g., mindful breathing, body scan, mindful walking)

_____

_____

When and where will I practice? (e.g., before bed in my room, during my lunch break)

_____

_____

Week 9: Almost There!

You're in the home stretch! Can you believe how much you've grown over the past few weeks?

Keep up the momentum! Now is the time to really focus on those goals, solidify those habits, and make B.A.D. Decisions a part of your everyday life.

Remember, this journey isn't just about reaching a destination; it's about transforming yourself along the way. Embrace the challenges, celebrate the victories, and never stop learning and growing.

You're almost there!

High five,

Coach Grace

Week 10:

M T W TH F S S

Weekly Affirmation Power-Up:
I am surrounded by love and support.
(Write it down every day this week and repeat it to yourself often.)

1. Goal Setting:

My Top Goal This Week: (Choose one goal to focus on first.)

_____

_____

Why is this goal important to me?

_____

_____

My SMART Plan:

- **S**pecific: (What exactly will I do?)

  _____

  _____

- **M**easurable: (How will I track my progress?)

  _____

  _____

- **A**chievable: (Is this goal realistic for me?)

  _____

  _____

- **R**elevant: (Does this goal align with my values and interests?)

  _____

  _____

- **T**ime-bound: (What is my deadline?)

  _____

  _____

Potential Obstacles: (What might get in my way?)

_____

_____

Solutions: (How will I overcome these obstacles?)

_____

_____

2. Habit Formation:

Habit I want to build this week: (e.g., exercise more, read every day, get enough sleep)

_____

_____

My Plan: (How will I make this habit a part of my routine?)

_____

_____

Tracking: (I will track my progress by...)

_____

_____

3. Time Management:

My Weekly Schedule: (I will create a schedule for my week that includes...)

_____

_____

My To-Do List: (My top 3 priorities this week are...)

1. _____

2. _____

3. _____

Time-Saving Tip: (One strategy I will use to be more efficient with my time is...)

_____

_____

4. Mindfulness Practice:

Mindfulness Technique I will try this week: (e.g., mindful breathing, body scan, mindful walking)

_____

_____

When and where will I practice? (e.g., before bed in my room, during my lunch break)

_____

_____

Week 11:

Weekly Affirmation Power-Up:
I am grateful for my mistakes; they have helped me learn and grow.
(Write it down every day this week and repeat it to yourself often.)

1. Goal Setting:

My Top Goal This Week: (Choose one goal to focus on first.)

_____

_____

Why is this goal important to me?

_____

_____

My SMART Plan:

- **S**pecific: (What exactly will I do?)

  _____

  _____

- **M**easurable: (How will I track my progress?)

  _____

  _____

- **A**chievable: (Is this goal realistic for me?)

  _____

  _____

- **R**elevant: (Does this goal align with my values and interests?)

  _____

  _____

- **T**ime-bound: (What is my deadline?)

  _____

  _____

Potential Obstacles: (What might get in my way?)

_____

_____

Solutions: (How will I overcome these obstacles?)

_____

_____

2. Habit Formation:

Habit I want to build this week: (e.g., exercise more, read every day, get enough sleep)

_____

_____

My Plan: (How will I make this habit a part of my routine?)

_____

_____

Tracking: (I will track my progress by...)

_____

_____

3. Time Management:

My Weekly Schedule: (I will create a schedule for my week that includes...)

_____

_____

My To-Do List: (My top 3 priorities this week are...)

1. _____

2. _____

3. _____

Time-Saving Tip: (One strategy I will use to be more efficient with my time is...)

_____

_____

4. Mindfulness Practice:

   Mindfulness Technique I will try this week: (e.g., mindful breathing, body scan, mindful walking)

   _____

   _____

   When and where will I practice? (e.g., before bed in my room, during my lunch break)

   _____

   _____

Week 12:

Weekly Affirmation Power-Up:
I am proud of all I have accomplished.
(Write it down every day this week and repeat it to yourself often.)

1. Goal Setting:

My Top Goal This Week: (Choose one goal to focus on first.)

_____

_____

Why is this goal important to me?

_____

_____

My SMART Plan:

- **S**pecific: (What exactly will I do?)

  _____

  _____

- **M**easurable: (How will I track my progress?)

  _____

  _____

- **A**chievable: (Is this goal realistic for me?)

  _____

  _____

- **R**elevant: (Does this goal align with my values and interests?)

  _____

  _____

- **T**ime-bound: (What is my deadline?)

  _____

  _____

Potential Obstacles: (What might get in my way?)

_____

_____

Solutions: (How will I overcome these obstacles?)

_____

_____

2. Habit Formation:

Habit I want to build this week: (e.g., exercise more, read every day, get enough sleep)

_____

_____

My Plan: (How will I make this habit a part of my routine?)

_____

_____

Tracking: (I will track my progress by...)

_____

_____

3. Time Management:

My Weekly Schedule: (I will create a schedule for my week that includes...)

_____

_____

My To-Do List: (My top 3 priorities this week are...)

1. _____

2. _____

3. _____

Time-Saving Tip: (One strategy I will use to be more efficient with my time is...)

_____

_____

4. Mindfulness Practice:

Mindfulness Technique I will try this week: (e.g., mindful breathing, body scan, mindful walking)

_____

_____

When and where will I practice? (e.g., before bed in my room, during my lunch break)

_____

_____

Week 12: You Did It!

Congratulations, superstar! You've completed the 12-week B.A.D. Decisions journey!

Take a moment to celebrate this incredible accomplishment. You've learned, grown, and achieved so much.

But this isn't the end – it's just the beginning! You now have the tools and the mindset to create a life filled with purpose, joy, and success.

Keep making those B.A.D. Decisions, keep believing in yourself, and keep shining bright!

I'm so proud of you,

Coach Grace

www.ingramcontent.com/pod-product-compliance
Lightning Source LLC
LaVergne TN
LVHW021120080426
835510LV00012B/1776